For most of his career,
Nick da Costa
worked in advertising as a
copywriter and creative director for
several London ad agencies,
including his own.

But when he was approached by
a group of Dogs
to write up their dialogues,
he jumped at the opportunity.

What Dogs Really Talk About

Nick da Costa

First published in Great Britain in 2017
by Penright Publications
Wrestlingworth
Bedfordshire

A CIP catalogue record for this book is available
from the British Library

PB ISBN 978 1 9997328 0 6
EBOOK ISBN 978 1 9997328 1 3

Printed and bound in the UK

For Esther

In memory of Sammy, Leah,
Rufus, Tigger & Freddy

1. Origins

The Dogs were talking. As usual, they were sitting around the base of the old oak tree in the early evening.

There was Whitman, a Springer Spaniel, who - having been named after an American poet - affected an air of quiet superiority and tended to lead the discussion.

Anton, a Beagle, who rather fancied himself as Whitman's Number Two.

Then came Pippa, an exuberant and irrepressible Boxer bitch; Butch, a down-to-earth Staffordshire Bull Terrier; and Malcolm, a well-bred and quietly-spoken Red Setter.

Lastly there was Obi, a young Boxer, not long out of his puppy days.

This particular evening, their topic was *Evolution*.

"So how did we evolve?" asked Pippa, "I mean, there are so many different breeds."

"It's widely accepted," said Whitman, "that all Dogs are descended from Wolves."

"What are Wolves?" asked Obi.

"Think of them as German Shepherds who'd like to eat you," said Malcolm.

"No change there then," said Butch, but quietly, since he always felt just a tiny bit awed in the presence of dogs with names like Whitman and Anton. (*'Butch!'* for heaven's sake - what were his Owners *thinking of?*)

"But we don't all *look* like Wolves," said Pippa, "how did that happen?"

"Well," said Whitman, "in our *Great Project* to help the Owners, we specialised. Some of us grew large and powerful to tackle Wild Beasts - "

Pippa and Obi looked round the group proudly.

" - some of us developed enormous stamina to pursue Foxes and Deer - "

Anton beat his tail.

" - some of us developed terrific senses for flushing game birds and retrieving them - "

Whitman and Malcolm nodded to each other.

" - and some of us developed mighty chests and locking jaws to hold on in a tight spot and never let go."

Butch puffed out his chest.

"But whatever our individual differences - our *specialisations* - deep inside us all, there is still the *Inner*

Wolf – our Common Ancestor," concluded Whitman.

Pippa threw back her head and howled.

"Thank you, Pippa," said Whitman.

"There's a French Poodle, lives down our street," said Butch. "But I think he lost contact with his Inner Wolf some time ago"

2. Canis Lupus

The Dogs were talking. As usual, they were sitting around the base of the old oak tree in the early evening.

“I’ve been thinking more about the Wolf thing,” began Anton.

“How so?” Whitman asked.

“Well, I was wondering why some Wolves stayed in the Forest - and why some left it to join the Owners?”

Whitman thought for a moment.

“It had a lot to do with Fire, I believe,” he said.

“Fire? There’s nothing like a good fire,” said Pippa dreamily.

“Exactly my point,” Whitman continued. “It’s thought that some Wolves - more intelligent than the rest - realised that where there’s Fire - ”

“ - there’s warmth!” said Anton.

“ - and sausages!” added Butch.

“Well, not immediately, I suspect,” said Whitman, “but eventually.”

The group fell silent for a moment while they contemplated the pivotal role played by warmth and sausages in the historic co-operation of the two species.

“We helped the Owners hunt for game,” Whitman

continued, "- and they kept us warm and cooked our meat for us."

"The perfect arrangement," said Malcolm.

"Exactly," Whitman said. "It's why the proper name for Dogs is *Canis Lupus Familiaris.*"

"What's that?" Butch asked.

"It's Latin," Whitman answered.

"Please - what's Latin?" said Obi.

"Latin was the language spoken by the Ancient Romans."

"Who were they?" Pippa asked.

"They were a race of particularly clever Owners who named everything," Whitman replied.

"But what does it mean?" said Pippa.

"Well, roughly translated, Canis Lupus Familiaris means *Dog-Wolf belonging to a Household*. Or a shorter way of saying it might be *Family Dog-Wolf.*"

"Family Dog-Wolf!" repeated Pippa, banging her tail in delight.

"So… in a nutshell," Malcolm said, "Wolves went their way back into the Forest, and we went ours - '

" - onto the sofa!" concluded Butch.

3. Top Dog

The Dogs were talking. As usual, they were sitting around the base of the old oak tree in the early evening.

“Why are the Owners so excited at the moment?” Anton asked.

“They’re having an election,” answered Malcolm.

“What’s an election?” Obi asked.

“It’s when all the Owners get together and vote for who they want to be Top Dog,” Whitman explained.

“Like a Dog Show?” said Obi.

“Yes,” Malcolm replied, “but not so well-behaved.”

“And what happens when they’ve chosen their new Top Dog?” asked Anton.

“As far as I can tell,” said Whitman, “he or she does exactly what the previous Top Dog did.”

“If I were Top Dog,” said Pippa, “I’d immediately pass a Law giving all Dogs more treats.”

“It’s pretty much the same with the Owners,” Whitman said, “the new Top Dog always promises them more Treats - ”

“ - but somehow the Treats never appear,” Malcolm added.

"Don't the Owners get very angry about that?" Pippa asked.

"They do," Malcolm replied, "but then their new Top Dog just blames the previous Top Dog for eating them all."

"Democracy," said Whitman, "it's a wonderful thing."

4. Social Networking

The Dogs were talking. As usual, they were sitting around the base of the old oak tree in the early evening.

"This *Social Networking* thing is getting out of hand," said Malcolm.

"How so?" Anton asked.

"Well, the other day my Owner was so busy texting, he walked into a tree."

"Perhaps it's because Social Networking is still a novelty to them," Whitman said, "whereas we Dogs have always had it."

The others nodded. They knew exactly what he meant.

"Every time we mark a tree, a lamp-post or a wall we leave a complex chemical message that any other Dog can immediately understand."

"And the accumulation of these marks builds into an enormous body of knowledge," Malcolm added, "each Dog adding to it as he or she passes."

"Or pisses," said Butch, unable to resist.

"Thank you, Butch," said Whitman.

"I saw a programme about this once," Anton said, "and the Owners don't really understand it. They think we're just leaving our names, like a crude identity marker -"

" - whereas," Whitman continued, "we're passing on highly detailed information, not just about ourselves, but the latest news....births and deaths...cat sightings... good locations for squirrel chasing and, of course, the geographical co-ordinates of hundreds of other marking places."

"And the millions of receptors in our noses can decode all this in a flash," Malcolm added.

"So if the Owners had our sense of smell," Butch said, "they would never have needed their world-wide...what do they call it - ?"

"Internet," said Whitman.

"Is there a name for ours?" asked Obi.

"No need to name something that comes so naturally, that we Dogs instinctively understand," Whitman answered. "But if it needed a name, I believe I have a suggestion..."

The others waited.

"The Internose," said Whitman, proudly.

"I have another," said Malcolm, excited.

"Which is?" said Whitman, ever so slightly miffed.

"Nosebook."

5. May the Force be with you

The Dogs were talking. As usual, they were sitting around the base of the old oak tree in the early evening.

"So how did you come to be called Obi?" asked Anton.

"Actually, it's short for Obi-Wan Kenobi" asked Obi.

"Is that your Kennel name?" asked Whitman.

"No," said Obi, "I'm named after a Jedi knight."

"What's a Jedi knight?" asked Pippa.

"I'm not sure," replied Obi, "- but I think they happened a long time ago in a Galaxy far, far away."

This silenced the others for a moment.

"There are times - though not many - when I'm grateful I'm just called Butch," said Butch.

Just then, the moon came up over the hills behind the town.

"Ah, moonrise - " said Malcolm, " - always such a beautiful sight."

"I wouldn't be so sure - " said Obi, " - might be the Death Star."

6. Who was first?

The Dogs were talking. As usual, they were sitting around the base of the old oak tree in the early evening.

“Whitman, would you tell us more about The First Dog?” asked Obi politely.

“Of course,” Whitman replied, happy to be drawn on one of his favourite topics.

“As we all know,” he began, “the First Dog was really a Wolf, only this Wolf was a bit cleverer than the rest. While they were all off howling at the Moon, he - ”

“ - or *She*,” interrupted Pippa

“ - or *She*,” conceded Whitman, “was drawn to the circle of light where the Owners were huddled round their fire. Then, ever so slowly, he - ”

“- or *She*,” added Pippa.

“ - or *She* - crept closer until one of the Owners noticed him.”

“ - or *Her*,” said Pippa.

“ - or *Her*,” said Whitman through gritted teeth. “This particular Owner, wiser than the others, threw a piece of cooked meat to the Wolf who ate it up hungrily.”

“What kind of meat?” Anton asked.

“It doesn’t matter,” said Whitman, impatiently, “let’s say deer. Anyway - ”

“ - could have been bison,” suggested Malcolm.

“Alright, bison then. So, as I was saying - ”

“ - or wild boar,” said Butch, “I just love roast crackling.”

“ - it might even have been Sabre Tooth Tiger,” said Obi.

“Alright, alright,” said Whitman, “so the He-Wolf or She-Wolf ate up the cooked deer, bison, wild boar or Sabre Tooth Tiger and realised it was the best thing He or She had ever tasted.”

‘I love this story,” said Pippa, beating her tail, “Please go on.”

“Are you sure?” asked Whitman, a little icily.

“Yes, yes,” chorused the group.

“The next day,” Whitman continued, “when the Owners went hunting, the Wolf followed. And it could tell immediately that the Owners were looking in the wrong place. Its incredible sense of smell and its acute hearing told it that the game lay in another direction.”

“So what did it do?’

“It barked at the Owners, ran away a little distance, then stopped and barked again trying to get them to follow.”

“Did Wolves bark back then?" Anton asked.

“Good question,” said Malcolm, “I thought they howled.”

"It was a long time ago," replied Whitman tetchily, "there is no way of knowing for sure. Shall I go on?"

The rest all nodded eagerly.

"You're sure?'

They all nodded again.

"Very well," said Whitman, "the clever Wolf continued to...*howly-bark*...until the Owners realised what it wanted. So they followed and had their best day's hunting ever."

All the Dogs beat their tails.

"That night, the Clever Owner threw it some more cooked meat and the Wolf drew nearer to the wonderful warmth of the fire. And so it began: that first clever Wolf-Dog stayed with the Owners never to return to the wild."

"So it must have been a She-Wolf-Dog," said Pippa.

"How so?" said Whitman, for once a bit slow on the uptake.

"Well, if the clever Wolf-Dog *'stayed never to return to the wild'*, she must have had Puppies!" said Pippa, triumphantly.

7.Fashion

The Dogs were talking. As usual, they were sitting around the base of the old oak tree in the early evening.

Pippa arrived last. "How do I look?" she asked.

"Um…like you did yesterday?" Anton replied, "but why do you ask such a strange question?"

"Well," replied Pippa, "my Female Owner is always saying this to the Male one."

"Ah," said Whitman, "this must be all about *clothes*. You see, Owners are not as fortunate as we Dogs, born as we are with perfectly suitable coats. They have no natural covering."

"But why do they need so many?" Pippa asked. "My Female is always throwing open her wardrobe - which is totally *stuffed* with clothes - and saying *'I have nothing to wear,'* "

"I think," said Whitman, "you may be referring to *fashion*."

"What's fashion?" Butch asked.

Whitman thought for a moment.

"Fashion," he said finally, "seems to be a system the Owners evolved for making themselves unhappy about the clothes they already have."

The Dogs fell silent, marvelling at the sophistication of the Owners.

"I must confess to a sneaky liking for my Owner's cashmere sweater," said Butch.

"Cashmere sweater?" said Malcolm, shocked. "You don't wear it do you?"

"Of course not," Butch replied, looking ever-so-slightly offended, "but it makes great bedding."

8. Headlights

The Dogs were talking. As usual, they were sitting around the base of the old oak tree in the early evening.

"We were debating," said Whitman, "the issue of Cat Intelligence – and whether they have True Intelligence in any way we Dogs would recognise."

"There's no question they have Cunning - " added Anton, " - but is that necessarily the same thing?"

"Very interesting conundrum," said Whitman, "Is *Cunning* possible without *Intelligence*? Personally, I believe Kitty is a cleverly constructed bundle of automatic reflexes."

"Like a robot?" said Obi.

"Yes," added Malcolm, "but without the charm."

"Sad to say, but I think Owners consider them to be Intelligent," said Anton.

"It just goes to show how even The Owners can be fallible," said Whitman, "I have never understood how they can be taken in by Kitty."

"I think it may have something to do with their eyes," said Malcolm.

"How do you mean?" asked Butch.

"Well, a cat's eyes are somehow…unfathomable…" said Malcolm, "…hinting at hidden depths."

"Whereas," said Whitman, "it's really a case of *the headlights are on but there's nobody behind the wheel.*"

"I saw a TV programme once," said Pippa, "that showed how Ancient Egyptians used to worship Cats."

"Hard to believe," said Anton, shocked.

"They even had them Mummified," she added.

"Best use for a cat I've heard yet," growled Butch.

9. Driving

The Dogs were talking. As usual, they were sitting around the base of the old oak tree in the early evening.

"Owners and their cars," Whitman began, "now there's a study in itself: who drives, who sits where, choosing where to park – the arguments are endless."

"Where do you usually travel?" asked Malcolm.

"On a blanket on the back seat," said Whitman.

"Me, too," said Anton.

"Rear hatch," said Obi, "all to myself."

"Back seat," said Pippa, "but while my Owners are shopping, I always move into the driver's seat."

"Why is that?" Whitman asked.

"I think it's important that other Owners see that there's someone in charge of the vehicle."

"Can you drive then?"

"No," Pippa replied, "but they don't know that, do they?"

10. Herding Sheep

The Dogs were talking. As usual, they were sitting around the base of the old oak tree in the early evening.

"One of the many things I resent about cats," began Anton, " - is they never do a stroke of work."

"Just so," agreed Whitman. "Ever since we left the forests to help the Owners, we Dogs have expected to *earn* our keep."

"A Point of Honour," said Malcolm, "the time-hallowed pact between Owner and Dog."

"But what has Kitty ever done?" said Butch, "Nothing."

"Can't fetch," said Pippa.

"More like won't," said Malcolm.

"Can't herd sheep," said Anton.

"Hardly surprising," said Whitman, "since the first requirement for herding sheep…" he paused briefly for effect, "…is to be cleverer than the sheep."

The Dogs all rolled onto their backs, waved their paws in the air and bayed with laughter.

"And the second - is to be feared by the sheep," added Malcolm. "I can't see any flock being much moved by Kitty running round going *Miaow, miaow!*"

Once again, the Dogs all rolled onto their backs, waved their paws in the air and bayed with laughter.

"And did you ever see a sign saying *Beware of the Cat*?" commented Butch.

"Or *Police Cats*, for that matter," said Anton, "Hard to imagine a police officer challenging a criminal with the warning *'Come quietly or I'll set the cat on you.'* "

"It's not for nothing we're known as Man's Best Friend," said Whitman, becoming serious. "We Dogs have always been ready to make the *Ultimate Sacrifice*: Loyal Unto Death. To us, Owners are *Everything*, whereas to Kitty - "

" - they're just a meal ticket," interrupted Anton.

"There is one thing cats are good for," said Pippa, excited.

"What's that?" Butch asked.

"Chasing."

11. Hunters

The Dogs were talking. As usual, they were sitting around the base of the old oak tree in the early evening.

"Whatever the truth about cat intelligence might be," said Whitman, "there is no question that *We* are the Senior Relationship."

"The *Special Relationship*," added Anton.

"A unique co-operation that enabled both our species to flourish," continued Whitman. "When Owners hunted we were right there with them - "

" - tracking down the herds - " said Butch.

" - retrieving small game - " said Malcolm.

" - cornering Wild Boars - " said Pippa.

" - catching Great Stags - " said Butch.

" - flushing out Woolly Mammoths!" said Obi, getting a little carried away.

"Very probably," said Whitman kindly.

"Mind you," said Butch, "Cats hunt, too."

"True," replied Whitman, "but I hardly think an occasional mouse on the mat puts them in quite the same league, do you?"

12. Balls

The Dogs were talking. As usual, they were sitting around the base of the old oak tree in the early evening.

Malcolm arrived last. He was carrying a bright yellow ball. The others looked at it enviously.

"Where did you get the Ball, Malcolm?" asked Butch, trying to keep his voice level.

"Borrowed it from some kids in the park," said Malcolm, a little evasively.

"Borrowed?" enquired Whitman gently.

"You mean the old *'join-in-and-then-run-off-with-it'* routine," said Butch. "Nice one, Malc."

"What is it about Balls?" said Whitman. "Why do we love them so much?"

"Could it be because they seem to have a life of their own?" said Anton.

"I think you may have hit on the truth of it," said Whitman, "in fact, I'm not certain that they aren't alive in some way"

"Some of them even squeak," said Obi. "Does that one squeak, please Malcolm?"

Malcolm tried it. "No," he said.

"Perhaps you killed the squeak," said Obi, "I do that all the time."

"My favourite is a Football," said Pippa. "I just love to join in the game."

"They don't mind you playing?" asked Malcolm.

"No, they *love* it when I play," said Pippa, "because that way they achieve the *Objective* of the game so much sooner."

"And what is that Objective?" enquired Whitman.

"Why - to puncture the ball, of course," said Pippa. " - *obviously*."

13. Collars

The Dogs were talking. As usual, they were sitting around the base of the old oak tree in the early evening.

Butch was the last to arrive, looking unusually pleased. The cause wasn't too hard to spot.

"New collar, Butch?" asked Whitman.

"Yes," said Butch proudly.

"Very fine," said Anton, "I especially like the studs."

"And the leather - it is leather isn't it? - is exactly your colour," added Malcolm.

"Funny things, collars," said Whitman, "I've never quite been able to decide whether they're a mark of servitude - or pride?"

"Interesting question," said Anton.

"In some ways, one could say they're both," suggested Malcolm. "Attached to a lead it's pretty clear who's boss."

"Not the way I pull," said Butch proudly.

"But equally," continued Malcolm, "I wouldn't want to be seen in public without one."

"I agree," said Pippa, who had a particularly fine one in Royal Blue. "A Dog on the street without a collar seems – somehow – *undressed*."

"There is, of course, the practical aspect," said Whitman, "- dog tags."

"How's that?" asked Butch.

"Well, our collars have tags with our name and telephone number, so if we get lost, other Owners know who to call."

"Why do we need them?" asked Butch.

"Possibly because we have yet to master the payphone?" suggested Whitman.

"I'm microchipped," said Obi suddenly.

"What does that mean?" asked Butch.

"I think it means I'm part dog, part computer," added Obi proudly.

"Yes," said Whitman, "I suspect that's entirely possible."

14. Chasing

The Dogs were talking. As usual, they were sitting around the base of the old oak tree in the early evening.

The topic was one they never tired of discussing.

“What do we most like to chase?” asked Whitman addressing his question to the group generally.

“Squirrels,” said Malcolm.

“Ever catch one?”

“No….but next time…”

“Birds,” said Obi.

“Ever catch one?”

“No…but almost…”

“Cars,” said Butch.

“Ever catch one?”

“No…but very, very nearly.”

“Cats,” said Pippa.

“Ever catch one?”

“No…but ever so close.”

“Rabbits,” said Anton.

“Ever catch one?”

"No…but it's just a question of time."

"I think there's a lesson here," concluded Whitman, "but I'm not quite sure what it is."

15. Advertising

The Dogs were talking. As usual, they were sitting around the base of the old oak tree in the early evening.

“One of the best things about sofas,” began Butch, “is being able to watch the television.”

“And do you have a favourite programme?” enquired Whitman.

“It’s one of those very short ones,” said Butch, “I think it’s called *Prime Chunks In A Delicious Gravy.*”

“I know that one,” said Pippa, excited, “it gets lots of repeats!”

“So tell us what happens,” asked Malcolm.

“Well,” said Butch, “it starts in a kitchen just as the Owners have come back from shopping. They have a big bag of groceries - ”

“ - that is such a *clever* opening,” said Pippa.

“Then they call their dog - ” said Butch, “ - who comes running in, all excited.”

“What kind of dog? asked Anton.

“A Lab,” said Butch.

“Not the most original casting then,” said Whitman. “I do so hate social stereotyping.”

“What happens next?” said Obi, excited.

"The Owners take a can out of the grocery bag, open it and spoon food into the Dog's bowl," said Butch, "and while this is happening you hear an Owner voice saying, "*Prime chunks of lean meat in a delicious gravy.*"

"Please, please, can I tell it now?" asked Pippa.

"If you must," said Butch.

"Because - next - there's this really *suspenseful* part where it looks as if the Owners are going to eat it themselves!"

"No!" said Anton.

"Yes!" said Pippa, "they smell it and all that."

"Weird," said Malcolm.

"But of course, in the end, they give it to their Dog and you've really never seen such big meaty chunks. And their Dog is very, very happy."

"My Owners actually bought me a can of it once," said Butch.

"And?" said Anton.

"Well, I found the delicious gravy - " said Butch, " - but I'm not sure what happened to the *prime chunks of lean meat.*"

"Aah," sighed Whitman, "The Power of Advertising."

16. Group Rules

The Dogs were talking. As usual, they were sitting around the base of the old oak tree in the early evening.

Obi arrived a little late, carrying a stick.

“Fine stick, Obi,” said Anton.

“Very fine stick,” agreed Butch.

Obi said nothing, due to the fact that he was still holding his stick.

“It’s alright to put the stick down,” said Whitman, “within *The Group* all property is sacred.”

Obi dropped the stick. “What about when the group breaks up?” he asked.

“How fast can you run?” said Malcolm.

17. Brightest

The Dogs were talking. As usual, they were sitting around the base of the old oak tree in the early evening.

"I was watching the stars last night," said Malcolm, "and there was one that was much brighter than the rest."

"Ah," Whitman said, "that would be Sirius, also known as the Dog Star."

"We have *our own star*?" asked Pippa, delighted.

"Of course," said Whitman. "The Early Owners gave names to all the most important stars and their constellations."

"What's a constellation?" Butch asked.

"A constellation is a *group* of stars," explained Whitman. "The Early Owners saw shapes in these groups and gave them names, too."

"So where is the Dog Star?" asked Anton.

"The Dog Star is in the constellation of Canis Major," said Whitman proudly. "If you look carefully, the stars there form the shape of a Dog."

"But what does *Canis Major* mean?" Pippa asked.

"It's Latin," said Whitman, "and - loosely translated - it means *Top Dog*."

All the Dogs beat their tails at this conspicuous evidence

of their importance to the Owners.

"And Canis Major is near to another constellation called Orion the Hunter," added Whitman.

"The Hunter and his Faithful Dog," said Pippa, even more delighted.

"So is there a constellation of the cat then?" Anton asked.

"Not in the earliest times," said Whitman. "But many thousands of years later there was a French astronomer who felt sorry for cats and thought they should have their own constellation."

"Obviously delusional," said Malcolm.

"Quite so," Whitman continued, "so for a time there was a constellation called Felis, which is Latin for cat."

"Just 'cat'?" asked Anton.

"Yes," said Whitman, "the astronomer wasn't *that* delusional."

"You said *for a time*," observed Malcolm.

"Yes," Whitman replied, "Modern astronomers considered it unimportant and it was discontinued. It's now obsolete."

"You have to respect the Owners," said Butch, "they know when they've made a mistake."

18. Walkies

The Dogs were talking. As usual, they were sitting around the base of the old oak tree in the early evening.

"While I love my Owners dearly," said Whitman, "there is one word they use that I really hate."

"Which is?" Malcolm asked.

"Walkies," replied Whitman.

"You mean you don't like walks?" Anton asked, astonished.

"On the contrary," said Whitman, "I love a walk - like all right-thinking Dogs. It's just the word itself: 'walkies' somehow trivialises a time-honoured custom central to the Owner/Dog Enterprise."

"Which is?" asked Butch.

"Hunting, of course," said Whitman. "Thousands and thousands of years ago, when the Owners picked up their spears in the frozen dawn, I somehow doubt that '*walkies*' was the call to their Dogs."

"Dog-Wolves," corrected Pippa, who could never get over the thrill of her ancestry.

"Indeed," said Whitman.

" – and She-Dog-Wolves," she added.

“Of course,” said Whitman, mastering his patience.

“What do you think they said, then?” Butch asked.

“Hard to be sure,” Whitman replied, “but it would have been something like ‘Time to hunt!’ or ‘Find game!’ ”

“Or maybe ‘Let’s do it!’ ” suggested Obi, who had been watching too many Action Movies.

“Possibly,” said Whitman.

“So what you’re saying,” said Malcolm, “is that ‘Walkies’ - forgive me - a *Walk* is really a *hunt*?”

“Exactly,” said Whitman. “The Owners may have forgotten, but we still have the incredible ears and noses of our Forebears.”

“Bears?” said Obi, a little confused, “I thought we were Wolves.”

“Ancestors then,” said Whitman, a trifle impatiently. “So - as I was saying - our senses remain finely tuned to the hunt…the spoor of deer…”

“…the tracks of rabbits,” added Pippa.

“…the snuffling of boars,” said Butch.

“…the Lair of the White Worm,” said Obi, who’d also been watching too many Horror Movies.

"Unlikely, but you never know," said Whitman kindly.

"Mind you," said Anton, "I often hear my Owners talking about hunting."

"Really?" said Malcolm, "what for?"

"Usually a parking space," replied Anton.

"That it should have come to this," sighed Whitman.

19. Cat Flaps

The Dogs were talking. As usual, they were sitting around the base of the old oak tree in the early evening.

"One of the many things I resent about cats," began Malcolm, "is cat-flaps."

"How so?" said Anton.

"Well, why should cats get to come and go as they please, when we Dogs have to ask to be let out or in?"

The group considered this injustice in silence for a few moments, then Butch spoke.

"Could it be," he said, "that a Dog-flap would leave rather a large hole in the door for bigger breeds?"

"He has a point there," said Pippa.

"I think, Malcolm," said Whitman finally, "that you may have got this the wrong way round."

"I have?" said Malcolm hopefully.

"When you think about it," continued Whitman, "the status is all *ours*: First, we use the *same door* as the Owners. Second, each time the Owners open the door *specially for us*, they are performing *a personal service.* As to an equal."

The others nodded, awed as ever by Whitman's insight.

"After all," said Whitman, "can you really see an Owner going to the trouble of opening *a whole door* – just for a cat?"

"I never thought of it like that," said Malcolm, thumping his tail, "but of course you are so right."

"Personally, I prefer one-way cat-flaps," said Butch, "the kind that let cats out…but don't let them back in."

"One-way cat-flaps?" said Anton, "I thought they all worked in both directions?"

"Not if you lie across them on the inside," said Butch with a big grin. "Such a rewarding *'thump!'* when Kitty comes rushing home for supper."

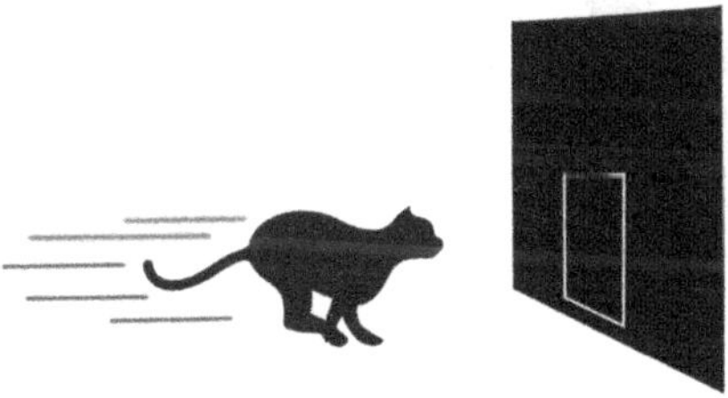

20. Who nose?

The Dogs were talking. As usual, they were sitting around the base of the old oak tree in the early evening.

"There was an animal expert on TV the other night," began Malcolm, "who said that we Dogs have no fewer than 300 million receptors in our noses, capable of detecting even the faintest of smells."

"How many devoted to Sausages?" Butch asked.

"In your case - " Whitman replied, "- about 300 million."

21. Four-legged friend

The Dogs were talking. As usual, they were sitting around the base of the old oak tree in the early evening.

"I was thinking," Whitman said, "that there is another animal whose relationship with the Owners comes close to our own."

"You can't mean cats, surely?" said Malcolm, shocked.

"Of course not," Whitman replied, "whatever it is between cats and their Owners could never be described as a *relationship*."

"More like a *transaction*," said Malcolm. "Owner gives. Cat takes. End of."

"Precisely," said Whitman. "No, the animal I was thinking of was the Horse. They've been helping the Owners almost as long as we have."

"Good point," Anton said. "Mind you, the Owners have never taken them into their homes like they have with us."

"I wonder if that might have something to with their great size?" said Malcolm.

"Not easy sharing a sofa with a Horse,' added Pippa, wisely.

"There is something very straight about Horses,"

Whitman continued, "and they can talk you know, in their own way."

"Can you talk Horse?" Butch asked.

"Only if I have a sore throat," answered Whitman, rolling onto his back and waggling his paws at his own wit.

"Sorry, about that," he said, collecting himself, "couldn't resist."

"So have you ever talked with a Horse?" Anton pressed.

"Yes," Whitman replied, "there's one we see on one of our walks and I sometimes stop to pass the time of day. But you have to understand their conversation is quite limited - nothing like ours."

"So what does the Horse talk about?" asked Obi.

"Apples, mostly," said Whitman.

22. Kids

The Dogs were talking. As usual, they were sitting around the base of the old oak tree in the early evening.

Anton had news.

“There’s a baby on the way,” he announced.

“Ah,” said Malcolm, “you’ll have to tread carefully now.”

“How so?”

“Because you’ll no longer be The Favourite,” Whitman explained, “time to take a back seat.”

“The trick,” said Malcolm, “is always stay close to the kids. *‘Look at how good Malcolm is with the children,’* my Owners say, *‘always guarding them.’* ”

“Which is, of course, no more than the truth,” Whitman added, “but not necessarily the *whole* truth.”

“Which is?” Pippa asked.

“Kids always drop a lot of food,” said Malcolm.

23. Evolutionary Tree

The Dogs were talking. As usual, they were sitting around the base of the old oak tree in the early evening.

"How did Owners come to be *Number One*?" asked Anton, "speaking from an evolutionary perspective?"

Whitman thought about this for a moment. "Brains, pure and simple," he said. "They were always the smartest breed on the planet."

"So who is Number Two?" asked Obi.

"Why, Dogs of course," said Whitman, "without a shadow of a doubt."

"I thought Apes were considered next-in-line on the Evolutionary Tree," said Malcolm.

"That's a common misconception," replied Whitman, "based, I believe, on their superficial resemblance to Owners. But I ask you: if they were really that smart, would they still be living in trees without a roof over their heads?"

The others nodded in agreement.

"So where do cats come then?" asked Pippa.

"Somewhere close to Goldfish, would be my guess," said Butch.

The Dogs rolled onto their backs, waved their paws and bayed with laughter.

“Come now,” said Whitman, “I think that’s being a little bit unfair – ” he paused for a second, “ – on Goldfish!”

Once again, the Dogs rolled onto their backs, waved their paws in the air and bayed with laughter.

“They say cats have nine lives,” said Pippa.

“When you’re that dim, you need them,” answered Butch.

24. Special Skills

The Dogs were talking. As usual, they were sitting around the base of the old oak tree in the early evening.

"I saw a Guide Dog walking his Owner down our street this morning," Malcolm said.

"A wonderful sight," said Anton, "an Owner trusting a Dog to be his eyes."

"Trust is the word," said Whitman. "It's Trust that lies at the very heart of the relationship between Owners and Dogs. After all, a Dog that can't be trusted - "

" - is probably a cat in disguise," interrupted Butch.

The Dogs all rolled onto their backs, waggled their paws in the air and bayed with laughter.

"Of course," continued Whitman, collecting himself, "A Guide Dog is just one of many *Career Dogs* the Owners rely on."

"What's a Career Dog?" Obi asked.

"A Career Dog is one who has developed Special Skills to help the Owners," Whitman answered.

"Such as?" said Pippa.

"Sheepdogs?" suggested Malcolm.

"Sheepdogs are a good example," agreed Whitman, "an Owner could never cover the ground fast enough to herd a flock of sheep."

" - and they're no good at growling," added Butch.

"Precisely," said Whitman.

"What about Sniffer Dogs?" said Malcolm.

"Another good example," said Whitman.

"But all Dogs can sniff," Pippa said.

"Of course," said Whitman, "but these are Dogs who have been trained to sniff for very specific things."

"Like what?" asked Pippa.

"Drugs, for one," said Malcolm.

"What are drugs?" Obi asked.

"Drugs are substances some Owners take to make themselves feel happier," Whitman explained.

"Must be Owners who don't have a Dog," Pippa said.

"I suspect that's very true," Whitman agreed.

"Then there are Sniffer Dogs trained to find explosives," said Malcolm.

"What do they do when they find them?" asked Anton.

"Run?" suggested Butch.

"But don't we all have the same gifts as these Career

Dogs?" Anton asked.

"Of course," said Whitman, "and should the Call ever come, I'm sure we would all rise to the challenge."

"*I'm* a Career Dog," announced Butch.

"You are?" said Whitman, "what kind?"

"A *Sofa Dog*," said Butch proudly.

"And were you trained specially for this Task?"

"No," said Butch. "It just comes naturally."

25. Separation Anxiety

The Dogs were talking. As usual, they were sitting around the base of the old oak tree in the early evening.

“Have any of you been watching that documentary series about Dogs?” Anton asked.

The rest of the group nodded, all except for Obi who preferred the sci-fi channel.

“Did you see the one about *Separation Anxiety*?”

They all nodded again.

“In my opinion, it really let the series down. They couldn’t have got it more wrong if they’d tried,” he continued.

“Right name, wrong diagnosis,” Malcolm added.

“A classic case of drawing the wrong conclusions from circumstantial evidence,” Whitman said.

“What’s Separation Anxiety?” Obi asked.

“It’s when we Dogs show signs of stress and anxiety whenever our Owners go out,” said Malcolm.

“But some of us do,” said Pippa.

“But not for the reasons they think,” said Anton.

“They think we can’t handle being alone,” Whitman said, “but the real reason we’re anxious...*is for them*.”

"Exactly," said Malcolm. "I'm never confident my Owner can even find his way home without help. Once, he even drove to their previous house."

"And mine is always losing her keys, her mobile phone, her handbag..." said Butch, "I shudder every time she goes out."

"My two even lost their Little One in a department store and couldn't find him for twenty minutes! Any one of us would have sniffed him out in seconds!" Anton said.

"The fact is, they can't be totally trusted on their own," Whitman added. "For eons we Dogs have kept them out of trouble: warning them of dangers, making up for their hopeless senses of hearing and smell. An Owner on the loose without a Dog is an accident just waiting to happen."

They all nodded at the truth of this.

"And when we give them the big welcome on their return, they think we're just overjoyed to see them, but it's not really that, is it?"

The others shook their heads.

"What is it, then?" Obi asked.

"Surprise."

26. IQ

The Dogs were talking. As usual, they were sitting around the base of the old oak tree in the early evening.

"Interesting programme on Dog Training last night," said Anton.

"I missed it," said Whitman, "what happened?"

"Well, the Owners set up a kind of test," Anton explained.

"They do love their tests," Malcolm said. "Which one was this?"

Anton continued:

"There were two rows of treats forming a kind of course, with the Dog at one end and the Owner at the other. The idea being that - when the Owner called - the well-trained Dog would ignore the treats and run straight to the Owner."

"Fascinating," said Whitman.

"How many treats?" Pippa asked, "these details are important."

"Must have been eight or so," Anton said.

"A really challenging test, then," said Pippa.

"But what happened?" asked Malcolm, impatiently.

“Well, the first Dog ran straight to its Owner and got a treat.”

“Definitely a well-trained Dog,” said Pippa.

“But the second Dog,” Anton continued, “totally ignored the Owner’s call and systematically ate up all the treats.”

“All eight of them?” asked Pippa.

“Every one,” Anton replied, “and all the Owners laughed.”

Whitman sighed.

“It’s always sad when a Dog lets the side down,” he said.

“Too true,” said Malcolm. “That first Dog was as stupid as it gets.”

“One treat instead of eight,’ said Pippa, shaking her head sadly. “Couldn’t do the maths.”

27. Harmony?

The Dogs were talking. As usual, they were sitting around the base of the old oak tree in the early evening.

"I've been thinking about one of *The Great Questions*," Whitman said. "Can a Dog live in harmony with a cat?"

Malcolm turned to Butch who, as they all knew, was forced to *live in shame*, "Butch, are you OK with this?"

"No problem," replied Butch gruffly, "it helps to talk."

"So how do you manage things?" Anton asked.

Butch was thoughtful for a moment.

"You have to remember," he said, "that there some Owners - mine for one - who actually like cats."

The Dogs all shook their heads in disbelief.

"Hard to believe that the most intelligent species on the planet can be so easily fooled," said Anton.

"I put it down to *Low Self-Esteem*," said Whitman, "there must be some Owners who simply like to be ignored."

"You are so right," said Pippa, "a welcome from a Dog is *A WELCOME*. But a welcome from a cat is - "

" - undetectable?" added Whitman.

"Well-put," Malcolm said, "Kitty doesn't care who comes

through the front door so long as they can use a can opener."

"And what help would Kitty be if that person was a burglar, I ask?" said Butch, "None at all."

"The other day I was watching a film about a Cat Burglar," Pippa declared.

"Is that someone who steals cats?" Obi asked.

"Sadly, no," Whitman replied.

"So how do you manage things, Butch?" Anton asked.

"You have to be clever about it," said Butch, "and suppress your natural instinct to chase it up the nearest tree. So occasionally, when the Owners aren't looking, I eat Kitty's food."

"What's cat food like?" asked Obi.

"Not great," replied Butch, "but knowing Kitty's not getting any lends a lot to the taste."

28. Final Frontier

The Dogs were talking. As usual, they were sitting around the base of the old oak tree in the early evening.

"Today is a very special day," Whitman said.

"Did you have steak for supper then?" Anton asked.

"No, not that. Today - ," Whitman paused briefly to underline the importance of his announcement, " - is the anniversary of the first animal from Earth to travel into space."

"Which was?" chorused the Group.

"Why, a Dog, of course."

"What was his name?" asked Butch.

"It wasn't a He," replied Whitman, "it was a *She*."

Pippa beat her tail in delight.

"What was her name?" she asked.

"Laika," said Whitman, "and the Russians gave her the great honour of being the first creature from Earth to leave the planet."

"What happened?" Malcolm asked.

"She completed several orbits of the earth, but eventually her oxygen ran out and she did not survive the journey."

“Was it a one-way mission, then?” Anton asked.

“I fear so,” Whitman replied.

There was silence for a moment as the Group reflected on the Heroism of Laika.

“Should have sent a cat,” growled Butch.

“Nonsense,” said Whitman, “a cat could never master the sophisticated control systems of a spacecraft.”

The Group nodded at the obvious truth of this.

“No,” continued Whitman, “when it came to it, the Russians realised that there could be no better Ambassador for our planet than a Dog.”

“Right,” said Obi, “she could have run into Klingons…or even the Borg.”

“I think you may be spending too much time in front of the television, Obi,” said Whitman gently.

29. Use of Tools

The Dogs were talking. As usual, they were sitting around the base of the old oak tree in the early evening.

"I've been thinking more about how the Owners came to be the dominant species," began Whitman.

"And what are your conclusions?" Anton asked.

"I think you have to put it down to their sheer *inventiveness*," said Whitman.

" - plus their use of tools?" suggested Malcolm.

"Exactly," said Whitman. "When you combine inventiveness with the skill to make things, there's no end to the possibilities."

"Mind you," said Anton, "Apes have been shown to be both inventive and to use tools."

"Granted," said Whitman, "but I think it unlikely we'll be seeing a washing machine designed and built by Apes anytime soon."

"So what do you consider to be the high points of the Owners' creations?" Malcolm asked.

"Well, aeroplanes would have to come high on the list," said Whitman. "To conquer the air itself is a remarkable achievement."

"How about the Motor Car?" suggested Pippa.

"That, too," said Whitman.

"The AH64-D Apache attack helicopter," said Obi, who'd been following a TV series on military hardware.

"An achievement, certainly," said Whitman, after a brief hesitation.

"Computers," proposed Malcolm.

"Undoubtedly," said Whitman, then turned to Butch who had taken no part in the discussion so far, "What do you think Butch?"

"Well, I've been listening to all the other suggestions and thinking hard," said Butch.

"And?" chorused the rest.

"I've narrowed it down to two," he said.

"Which are?" they chorused again.

"The two *Esses*," said Butch.

"What are the two Esses?" asked Anton.

"Sausages," said Butch, "...and Sofas."

30. Festive Season

The Dogs were talking. As usual, they were sitting around the base of the old oak tree in the early evening.

“Christmas soon,” said Malcolm.

“I love Christmas,” said Pippa.

“Roast Turkey,” said Anton.

“Chipolatas,” said Butch.

“Smoked salmon” said Obi, whose Owners had made the mistake of introducing him to the finer things.

“Goose,” said Malcolm.

The group fell silent as they contemplated all the spiritual wonders of Christmas.

“One year, my Owners hung chocolates on the Christmas tree,” said Anton.

“That was thoughtful,” replied Butch.

“Yes, I thought so, too. Only it turned out they weren’t for me.”

“Ah,” said Whitman.

“Mind you,” Anton continued, “I’d cleared most of the lower branches before they noticed.”

“Were they very cross?” Pippa asked.

“A bit. But it was Christmas, so it wasn’t too bad.”

“Lucky,” said Butch.

“In fact, I thought I’d got away with it…”

“You did?” said Pippa

“…but it was the empty wrappers that gave me away.”

“Ah,” said Whitman again.

“So the next year,” Anton continued, “they just hung them higher up the tree.”

“That’s exactly how Giraffes came to evolve their long necks,” said Whitman, “to reach the sweeter, juicier leaves at the top of the tree.”

“Do you think I could evolve a longer neck?” Anton asked.

“Not by this Christmas, I suspect,” said Whitman.

31. Guarding

The Dogs were talking. As usual, they were sitting around the base of the old oak tree in the early evening.

"This Owner/Dog thing," started Anton, "it's really quite complicated when you think about it."

"In what way?" asked Whitman

"Well, it's a bit like a contract isn't it? They do things for us - and we do things for them in return."

"So what kind of things do they do for us?" asked Butch.

"Feed us for one," said Malcolm

"Groom us," said Pippa

"That's a new one on me," said Butch

"We noticed," said Malcolm, but in a nice way.

"Take us for walks," said Obi

"We could do that by ourselves," said Anton

"Of course," said Malcolm, "but it's not quite the same thing. A walk with an Owner is *A Walk* but a walk *without* an Owner is..."

"Lost?" suggested Whitman.

"I know the most important thing we do for them," said Pippa, excited.

“Which is…?” said Whitman.

“Guarding!” said Pippa.

“You’re right!” said Malcolm, “without us, they’d be helpless.”

“How so?” asked Anton.

“Well, for one, they have useless ears. Can’t hear anything until it’s right on top of them. We’re their *Early Warning System.*”

“Exactly,” said Butch, “every day there’s a man who stuffs paper through our front door – and they’ve never heard him coming yet. I do my best to warn them, but they don’t seem to mind.”

“Will you tell him, or shall I?” asked Whitman, speaking to no one in particular.

32. Vets

The Dogs were talking. As usual, they were sitting around the base of the old oak tree in the early evening.

“Vets,” said Anton, “I’m never sure whether to lick them or bite them.”

“When they put on those rubber gloves,” Butch replied, “teeth is best.”

“Come now,” said Whitman, “Vets only have our best interests at heart.

“How come mine always seem to be at the rear?” Butch asked.

“Vets are proof how much our Owners care for us,” Whitman continued, “They have their doctors…we have our vets.”

“What’s the difference between a doctor and a vet?” Obi asked.

“I believe vets get paid more,” said Whitman, “probably because they have to treat all kinds of animals."

“Even cats?” Anton asked.

“Even cats.”

“Cats don’t need a vet,” said Malcolm, “they need a psychiatrist.”

"I guess that's why their Owners have to bring them in baskets," Anton said, "because they can't be trusted to behave."

"Basket cases, the lot of them," growled Butch.

"I saw an old mate of mine at the vets the other day," said Anton. "Funny thing: he went in with his Owner, but only the Owner came out."

"Perhaps they had a special exit, just for Dogs?" said Pippa.

"Something like that," said Whitman quietly.

33. Showtime

The Dogs were talking. As usual, they were sitting around the base of the old oak tree in the early evening.

"Did anyone watch Crufts last night?" Whitman enquired.

The rest all nodded, with the exception of Butch.

"I was watching The Jewellery Channel," he explained, a little embarrassed.

"The Jewellery Channel?" said Malcolm, "not your sort of thing I'd have thought?"

"My Owners were out," Butch explained, "so it's always a bit hit-and-miss with the controller, as we all know."

"True," said Whitman, "until the Owners design a paw-friendly remote, we're at a distinct disadvantage."

"Mind you, I saw a very nice pair of diamond ear studs," said Butch, then quickly added "that I...*imagine*...would have been perfect for my female Owner."

There was a brief silence while the group digested this sophisticated new aspect to Butch.

"So what did the rest of us think about Crufts?" Whitman continued.

"Always fascinating to witness the Owners' obsession with qualities that are irrelevant to any right-thinking Dog," Malcolm said.

"Exactly," said Pippa, "a good nose is a good nose, no matter what kind of Dog it's attached to."

"A wagging tail doesn't care what precedes it," added Anton.

"I think the obsession with appearance," said Whitman, "might be more acceptable if the Owners applied the same rigorous standards to themselves. But the Arena has always struck me as something of a fashion backwater."

"They spend hours grooming their Dogs to perfection," Malcolm continued, "then stroll on looking like they dressed in the dark."

"In fact, were aliens to tune in to the show," said Anton, "they might easily be confused as to which is the dominant species."

"I was in a show once," said Butch quietly.

"You were?" chorused the others, surprised at yet another revelation.

"Just a little local show. I won best in category."

"And what category was that?" Whitman asked.

"*Most Beautiful Puppy*," said Butch shyly.

There was the briefest of pauses.

"Who could doubt that for a second?" said Malcolm warmly, "well-done Butch."

"Did you get a prize?' Pippa asked.

"I got a big blue rosette," said Butch glumly.

"How lovely," said Pippa.

"Not really," said Butch. "I'd have preferred a sausage."

34. Alive?

The Dogs were talking. As usual, they were sitting around the base of the old oak tree in the early evening.

"I'm still not sure about the vacuum cleaner," Anton said.

"In what way?" asked Malcolm.

"Well, I know it's one of the Owners' clever machines, but I still get the feeling it has a life of its own."

"I know exactly what you mean," Whitman said, "I have the same suspicions about the lawnmower."

"The really cunning one is the washing machine," said Butch. "One minute it goes silent, then the next – just as you're walking past – it roars at you."

"That's why I always bark at the vaccuum," Anton said, "just to be on the safe side."

"Same goes for the lawnmower," said Whitman, "it's important to let these machines know who's boss."

"My Owners have a *robot* vacuum cleaner," said Obi, proudly.

"A *robot* vacuum cleaner? What's that?" Butch asked.

"It's a special kind that doesn't need an Owner to push it," Obi replied.

"You mean it moves by itself?" Pippa asked.

"Yes. It can be sitting there by the wall, all quiet, then suddenly it wakes up and goes to work."

"That must be terrible!" Anton said.

"No, it's great!" said Obi, "we're good friends. When the Owners are out, we play Tag."

35. Obedience

The Dogs were talking. As usual, they were sitting around the base of the old oak tree in the early evening.

“I was wondering,” said Anton, “about the Obedience thing.”

“How do you mean?” asked Whitman.

“Well, why are Owners so obsessed with it? And - more to the point - why do *we* fall for it?”

Whitman thought for a while.

“I think it is has something to do with control. It makes them feel better.”

“It’s a bit rich,” said Malcolm, “Controlling us when they can’t even control their own children.”

“Good point,” said Butch, “If I behaved the way my Owners’ kids do, I’d be in the…er…the…er…what’s the word I’m looking for?”

“Doghouse?” suggested Whitman

“Exactly.”

“But why do we fall for it?” said Anton. “We’re our own Dog, unique and individual. Wildness is in our DNA.”

“I think,” said Whitman, “it may have something to with treats.”

“Treats?” said Pippa, lifting her head, “Where?”

"It goes back to puppyhood," continued Whitman. "*Sit!* Get a treat. *Come!* Get a treat! *Heel!* Get a treat. You know how it goes."

"Before long," added Malcolm, "it's automatic."

"There was once a Russian Owner called Pavlov, who made a study of *Conditioned Reflexes* in Dogs," said Whitman.

"What was that all about?" Butch asked.

"He showed how a system of rewards and triggers could condition Dogs to behave in a certain way," Whitman said.

"Did he try it with cats?" Anton asked.

"Of course not," Whitman replied, "the tests were designed for an intelligent species."

"Well, maybe we should show more independence," said Anton, "we are, after all, free spirits."

Just then, a faint whistle could be heard on the evening breeze.

"That's me," said Anton, jumping up, "gotta go!"

And he was off in a blur.

"So much for free spirits," sighed Whitman.

If you've enjoyed this privileged insight
into What Dogs Really Talk About
you'll find lots more stuff at

www.whatdogstalkabout.com

You can also follow Whitman on Twitter:

Whitman @UpWithDogs